SUGAR FREE DESSERTS

Healthy and Delicious
Sugar Free Dessert Recipes

Olga Reed

TABLE OF CONTENTS

Introduction 1

Sugar-Free Apple Tart Recipe 2

Sugar-Free Chia Pudding 3

Sugar-Free Almond Butter Banana Cookies 4

No Sugar Cinnamon and Cardamom Fat Bombs 5

Sugar-Free Blueberry Ice Cream 6

Sugar-Free Fig Balls 7

No Sugar Banana Cookies 8

Superfoods Sugar-Free Protein Bars 9

Sugar-Free Banana, Peanut Butter Ice Cream 10

Sugar-Free Pomegranate- Goji Chia Pudding 11

Sugar-Free Peanut Butter Nuggets 12

No Sugar Apple Pie Bars 13

No Sugar Salty Coconut Treat 14

Sugar-Free Trifle 15

Sugar-Free Berry Mousse 16

Sugar-Free Strawberry Cheesecake Pie 17

Sugar-Free Creamy Cottage Cheese Pudding 19

Sugar-Free Grilled Peaches 20

Sugar-Free Coconut Vanilla Ice Cream 21

Sugar-Free Cantaloupe Ice Cream 22

Sugar-Free Strawberry Men 23

No Sugar Amazeballs 24

Sugar-Free Coconut Plantain Medallions 25

Sugar-Free Watermelon and Lemon Balm Sorbet 26

Sugar-Free Custard 27

Sugar-Free Chocolate Covered Strawberries 28

No Sugar Chocolate Cake 29

No Added Sugar Date Bars 30

Sugar-Free Peach Ice Cream 32

Sugar-Free Mousse au Chocolove 33

Sugar-Free Berry Frozen Yogurt 34

Sugar-Free Chocolate Chip Cookies 35

No-Sugar Avocado Chocolate Pudding 36

Conclusion 37

Your Free Gift

I would like to show you my appreciation for supporting my work so I've put together a free gift for you - **12 Green Cocktails Recipes**.

Email me at olgareedrecipes@gmail.com, type «**12 Green Cocktails Recipes**» in the subject line and I will send you my gift.

I know you will love this gift.

Thanks!

INTRODUCTION

When it comes to desserts, we desire both freshness and sweetness. The problem with standard desserts is they are loaded with added sugar. Everything we put in our bodies should nourish and improve our health. However, eating foods loaded with added sugar trigger weight gain and increase your risk of cardiovascular disease and diabetes. I have created this book to show you how to make delicious sugar free desserts without sacrificing flavor, taste or variety. Inside, you will discover 33 awesome, simple to make recipes that are designed to fit into your sugar-free lifestyle.

This inspiring book on Sugar Free Desserts: Healthy and Delicious Sugar Free Dessert Recipes, helps you remove all types of added sugar from your dessert recipes and an eye-opener for anyone who loves to treat family and friends with no sugar recipes. This book has been specially designed for individuals like you who desire to live and eat with as little added sugar as possible. If you have been searching for a way to follow the no sugar diet and live a healthier lifestyle, then this is the perfect no sugar dessert cookbook for you. All the recipes in this book are quick, easy and satisfy your need for delicious desserts. If you want to live a sugar-free lifestyle and want to know more, then read the book - 10-Day SUGAR DETOX: How to Stop Sugar Cravings on a Detox Diet - Quick Start Sugar Detox for Beginners with Healthy Diet Recipes by Olga Reed.

SUGAR-FREE APPLE TART RECIPE

Ingredients for 8 slices

- Premade pastry crust – 1 (9-inch, made with butter, flour, and salt)
- Thinly sliced sweet apples – 4 cups, skin removed
- Ground cinnamon – 1.5 tsp.
- Lemon juice – 2 tbsp.
- Unsweetened apple sauce – ¼ cup
- Cornstarch – 1 tbsp.

Method

1. Preheat the oven to 350F and spray a round tart pan (9.5-inch) with oil.
2. Press the pastry crust into the pan. Create the crust by folding down the edges and pressing into the sides of the pan. Keep in the refrigerator while you work with the other ingredients.
3. In a large bowl, mix together the cornstarch, apple sauce, lemon juice, cinnamon, and sliced apples. Toss and coat the apples evenly.
4. To the prepared crust, add the apple mixture in a pattern.
5. Bake until the edges of the tart are golden brown, about 35 to 40 minutes.
6. Cool completely and serve.

SUGAR-FREE CHIA PUDDING

Ingredients for 1 serving

- Coconut milk – ¾ cup
- Chia seeds – 2 tbsp.
- Vanilla extract – ½ tsp.

Method

1. In a glass jar, mix all the ingredients.
2. Cover and keep in the fridge overnight.
3. Before serving, make sure the pudding has thickened.
4. Serve the pudding with coconut milk, cream, and fresh berries.

SUGAR-FREE ALMOND BUTTER BANANA COOKIES

Ingredients for 12 cookies

- Mashed banana – ¼ cup
- Almond butter – ½ cup
- Quick oats – ¼ cup
- Vanilla extract – ¼ tsp.
- Salt – 1/8 tsp.

Method

1. Preheat the oven to 325F.
2. In a bowl, stir together all the ingredients. On prepared baking sheet, drop spoonfuls of batter about 1 inch apart. Flatten as desired.
3. Bake in preheated oven until cookies are firm to the touch, about 7 to 9 minutes.
4. Cool on the baking sheet for 5 minutes, then transfer to a cooling rack.
5. Serve.

NO SUGAR CINNAMON AND CARDAMOM FAT BOMBS

Ingredients for 10 servings

- Unsalted butter – 3 oz.
- Unsweetened shredded coconut – 5 tbsp.
- Ground cardamom – 1 pinch
- Vanilla extract – ¼ tsp.
- Ground cinnamon – 2 pinches

Method

1. Bring the butter to room temperature.
2. Carefully roast the shredded coconut until they turn a little brown.
3. In a bowl, mix the spices, butter, and half of the shredded coconut.
4. With two tsp. form into walnut-sized balls. Roll in the rest of the shredded coconut.
5. Store in the freezer.

SUGAR-FREE BLUEBERRY ICE CREAM

Ingredients for 6 servings

- Heavy whipping cream – 1 cup
- Egg yolks – 3
- Ground cardamom (green) – ½ tsp.
- Zest of ½ lemon
- Mascarpone cheese – 8 oz.
- Blueberries – 6 oz. frozen

Method

1. Remove the blueberries from the freezer.
2. In a bowl, whip the cream until soft peaks form and set aside.
3. In another bowl, beat vanilla, egg yolks, cardamom and lemon zest until pale and fluffy.
4. Mix in the cheese and then fold in the whipped cream.
5. When the blueberries are half-thawed, fold them into the mixture.
6. In a container, add the mixture and cover with a lid. Place in the freezer.
7. Stir the mixture every 15 minutes until it firms up.
8. Serve after 2 hours.

SUGAR-FREE FIG BALLS

Ingredients for 12 balls

- Raw shelled sunflower seeds – ½ cup
- Dried figs – 10 (stems removed)
- Zest and juice of 1 lemon
- Cardamom – ¼ tsp.
- Sunflower seeds – 2 tbsp. (for coating)

Method

1. Pulse 2 tbsp. sunflower seeds in a food processor until the consistency is almost flour like. Do not over process. Pour into a bowl and set aside.
2. In a food processor, place the cardamom, lemon juice, lemon zest, figs, and ½-cup sunflower seeds. Processes until it becomes dough like.
3. Roll about 1 tbsp. dough into a ball. Repeat with the rest of the dough.
4. Roll each ball into the processed sunflower seed flour.
5. Serve.

NO SUGAR BANANA COOKIES

Ingredients for 36 cookies

- Bananas – 3 ripe
- Rolled oats – 2 cups
- Dates – 1 cup, pitted and chopped
- Vegetable oil – 1/3 cup
- Vanilla extract – 1 tsp.

Method

1. Preheat the oven to 350F.
2. Mash the bananas in a bowl. Stir in oil, dates, oats, and vanilla.
3. Mix well and set aside for 15 minutes.
4. On to an ungreased cookie sheet, drop by teaspoonfuls.
5. In the preheated oven, bake until lightly brown, about 20 minutes.
6. Cool and serve.

SUPERFOODS SUGAR-FREE PROTEIN BARS

Ingredients for 8 large or 20 mini

- Chia seeds – 1/3 cup
- Coconut flakes – ¼ cup
- Hemp seeds – ¼ cup
- Hemp or pea protein powder – 2 cups
- Dates – 2 cups
- Cocoa powder – 3 tbsp.
- Water – ½ cup
- Mixed nuts – 1 cup
- Sunflower seeds – ½ cup

Method

1. In a food processor, mix dates and water and process until becomes a smooth paste.
2. Add all ingredients and blend until paste, about 15 seconds.
3. Blend and mix completely.
4. Cover a pan with parchment paper and press the batter into the pan.
5. Let sit overnight.
6. Cut and serve.

SUGAR-FREE BANANA, PEANUT BUTTER ICE CREAM

Ingredients for 4 servings

- Bananas – 5 ripe, peeled and frozen
- Peanut butter – ¼ cup, or any nut butter
- Cocoa powder – ¼ cup
- Vanilla extract – 1 tbsp.
- Pinch of sea salt
- Optional: cocoa nibs, roasted peanuts, chocolate chips, sliced bananas

Method

1. 1 day before you decide to make the recipe, cut the bananas into quarters and freeze them.
2. Remove the bananas from the freezer and place into the food processor.
3. Add vanilla, sea salt, cocoa powder, and peanut butter, cover with the lid and process until the mixture gets stuck in the food processor.
4. Stop and scrape down the sides, then process until mixture become a creamy smooth ice cream.
5. Place in the freezer for a few hours to create a firmer texture.
6. Serve.

SUGAR-FREE POMEGRANATE-GOJI CHIA PUDDING

Ingredients for 2 servings

- Unsweetened almond milk – 2 cups
- Fresh pomegranate arils – 2 cups
- Whole chia seeds – 2 tbsp.
- Ground chia seeds – 2 tbsp.
- Dried goji berries – ½ cup

Method

1. Into a blender, combine pomegranate arils, almond milk, ground and whole chia seeds and process until smooth.
2. Pour into a medium bowl and stir in the goji berries.
3. Place in the refrigerator overnight to set.
4. Stir and serve.

SUGAR-FREE PEANUT BUTTER NUGGETS

Ingredients for 30 nuggets

- Natural peanut butter – ½ cup
- Nonfat dry milk powder – ¼ cup
- Unsweetened flaked coconut – ¼ cup
- Rolled oats – 1/3 cup
- Ground cinnamon – ½ tsp.
- Wheat germ – ¼ cup
- Unsweetened apple juice concentrate, - ¼ cup, thawed

Method

1. In a large mixing bowl, combine coconut, milk powder, and peanut butter.
2. Stir in apple juice concentrate, wheat germ, ground cinnamon, and oats.
3. Shape the mixture into 1-inch balls.
4. Chill overnight and serve.

NO SUGAR APPLE PIE BARS

Ingredients for 12 bars

- Crushed almonds – 1 ½ cups
- Dates – 2 cups
- Dried apples – 1 ½ cups (grind very finely)
- Walnuts – 1 cup (grind up coarsely)
- Cinnamon – 3 tsp.

Method

1. Very finely grind the almonds in a food processor and place them in a large bowl.
2. Then grind down the dates into a paste. Add the almonds and mix well.
3. Add dried ground apple to the bowl. Then add the ground walnuts to the bowl. Add the cinnamon and mix well.
4. Into a 9x9 pan, pour the mixture evenly and cover with plastic wrap or parchment paper.
5. Press down on the bars with your fingers until the whole pan is compressed.
6. Chill in the refrigerator for 1 hour and cut into bars.

NO SUGAR SALTY COCONUT TREAT

Ingredients for 10 servings

- Dark chocolate – 3 ½ oz. with at least 70% cocoa solids
- Walnuts, pecan nuts, or hazelnuts – 10 pieces
- Roasted unsweetened coconut chips – 2 tbsp.
- Pumpkin seeds – 1 tbsp.
- Sea salt

Method

1. Melt the chocolate in the microwave oven.
2. Bring out 10 small cupcake liners (about 2 inches in diameter).
3. Add the chocolate to the cupcake liners.
4. Add the seeds, coconut chips, nuts and a few salt flakes.
5. Let cool and serve.

SUGAR-FREE TRIFLE

Ingredients for 4 servings

- Avocado – 1 ripe
- Banana – ½ ripe
- Coconut cream – ¾ cup
- Lime juice – 1 tbsp. and some of the zest
- Vanilla extract – 1 tbsp.
- Fresh raspberries – 3 oz.
- Pecan nuts – 2 oz. roasted

Method

1. In a bowl, mix together coconut cream, banana, avocado and ½ the vanilla. Separately mix the berries and remaining vanilla.
2. Fill dessert glasses with alternating layers of the two mixtures.
3. Top with roasted nuts and serve.

SUGAR-FREE BERRY MOUSSE

Ingredients for 8 servings

- Heavy whipping cream – 2 cups
- Fresh blueberries, or raspberries or strawberries – 3 oz.
- Chopped pecan nuts – 1 ¾ oz.
- Zest of ½ lemon
- Vanilla extract – ¼ tsp.

Method

1. Into a bowl, pour the cream and whip with a hand mixer until soft peaks form. Add the vanilla and lemon zest towards the end.
2. Add the nuts and berries to the whipped cream and stir thoroughly.
3. Cover with plastic wrap and keep in the refrigerator overnight.
4. Serve.

SUGAR-FREE STRAWBERRY CHEESECAKE PIE

Ingredients for 8 servings

- Crust
- Raw sunflower seeds – ¾ cup
- Shredded coconut – ¾ cup
- Salt – ¼ tsp.
- Powdered stevia – 1 tbsp.
- Butter – 3 tbsp.

Filling

- Sliced strawberries – 2 cups
- Lemon juice – 1 ½ tsp.
- Salt – ¼ tsp.
- Liquid lemon stevia – 1 tsp.
- Light cream cheese – 18 ounce, softened
- Heavy cream – 1 cup
- Vanilla liquid stevia – ½ tsp.

Method

1. Grind the coconut, sunflower seeds, stevia and salt until fine crumbs.
2. Gradually add melted butter and process until combined.
3. Into the bottom and up sides of a 9-inch pie pan, press mixture then set aside.
4. In a blender, add lemon juice, strawberries, liquid stevia, and salt.
5. Blend until pureed.
6. Whip cream cheese in a stand mixer until smooth and no clumps.

7. Pour in vanilla stevia and heavy cream and blend on high until whipped.
8. Into the whipped cream cheese mixture, pour the pureed strawberries and blend until mixed well.
9. Pour the mixture into pie crust, cover and freeze overnight.

SUGAR-FREE CREAMY COTTAGE CHEESE PUDDING

Ingredients for 6 servings

- Cottage cheese – 2/3 lb.
- Heavy whipping cream – 1 ¼ cups
- Vanilla extract – 1 tsp.
- Ground cinnamon – 1 tsp.
- Fresh raspberries – 2 oz.

Method

1. In a bowl, whip the heavy cream until soft peaks form, then add the vanilla extract.
2. Gently fold in the cottage cheese, but don't over mix. Keep the pudding in the fridge for 20 minutes to settle.
3. Sprinkle with cinnamon and serve with raspberries.

SUGAR-FREE GRILLED PEACHES

Ingredients for 4 servings

- Ripe peaches – 3
- Butter or coconut oil – 2 tbsp.
- Ground cinnamon – 1 tsp.
- Heavy whipping cream – 1 cup
- Vanilla extract – ½ tsp.

Method

1. Cut the peaches into 4 pieces and remove the pits.
2. Brush oil or melted butter on the cut surface and grill the wedges in a grill pan or on an outdoor grill. About 1 minutes on each side. Also, you can use a frying pan to fry them.
3. In a bowl, whisk the whipping cream to soft peaks and stir in the vanilla.
4. Sprinkle with cinnamon and serve with whipped cream.

SUGAR-FREE COCONUT VANILLA ICE CREAM

Ingredients for 4 servings

- Full-fat (unsweetened) coconut milk – 2 cans
- Vanilla bean – 1

Method

1. Shake the can before opening.
2. On a rimmed baking sheet, place a sheet of parchment paper and pour the coconut milk onto the parchment paper.
3. Freeze until hard, about a few hours.
4. Once frozen, remove the coconut milk off the paper and break into chunks.
5. Add to the food processor and process until smooth. Scooping down the sides as necessary.
6. Add the vanilla seeds to the food processor. Process until you get your desired consistency.
7. Serve.

SUGAR-FREE CANTALOUPE ICE CREAM

Ingredients for 2 servings

- Cantaloupe melon – ¼
- Banana – 1

Method

1. Cut the cantaloupe and banana in pieces (remove the skin and seeds).
2. Place the pieces in a Ziploc bag and freeze them overnight.
3. Place the cantaloupe and banana pieces into your food processor and process until completely smooth.
4. Place the ice cream in the bowls and serve.

SUGAR-FREE STRAWBERRY MEN

Ingredients for 12 servings

- Strawberries – 12
- Apples – 3
- Unsweetened chocolate to taste
- Sliced almonds
- 1 melon baller (10 to 15 mm)
- Water
- Salt

Method

1. Cut the apple in half and scoop out the meat with a melon baller.
2. Submerge the apples in salted water to prevent from browning.
3. Then rinse under fresh water and drain.
4. In the microwave, melt the unsweetened chocolate.
5. Scoop out a hole from the strawberries with the melon baller.
6. With sliced almonds, make the mouth and make the eyes with melted chocolate.
7. Place the apple ball into the strawberry.
8. Line them up and serve.

NO SUGAR AMAZEBALLS

Ingredients 4 servings

- Banana – 1
- Coconut butter – 1/3 cup
- Raw carob powder – 2 tbsp.

Method

1. In a blow, mash banana with a fork. Mix in raw carob and coconut butter.
2. Roll spoonfuls of dough into a ball.
3. Keep in the fridge to harden.
4. Serve.

SUGAR-FREE COCONUT PLANTAIN MEDALLIONS

Ingredients for 4 servings

- Very ripe plantain – 1 large (ends cut and score the length of the skin lightly)
- Unsweetened coconut flakes – 1/3 cup
- Coconut oil – 2 tbsp.

Method

1. Peel the plantain and cut into ½-inch thick slices.
2. Pour coconut flacks into a bowl. Press the plantain slices into the bowl to coat both sides.
3. In a skillet heat coconut oil over medium high heat.
4. Fry the coated plantain slices in hot oil in a single layer.
5. Use a spatula to flatten them and cook 1 minute on each side.
6. Place on a plate, sprinkle with more coconut flakes and serve.

SUGAR-FREE WATERMELON AND LEMON BALM SORBET

Ingredients for 4 servings

- Watermelon – 2 cups
- Fresh lemon balm leaves – ¼ cup

Method

1. Cut and deseed the watermelon, then freeze.
2. In a food processor, combine frozen watermelon and lemon balm. Blend until smooth.
3. Serve.

SUGAR-FREE CUSTARD

Ingredients for 6 servings

- Eggs – 6
- Ripe bananas – 2
- Coconut milk – 1 can

Method

1. Preheat the oven to 350F.
2. Crack the eggs and add to a blender. Add the coconut milk and bananas. Blend.
3. In a large baking dish, place 6 half pint mason jars.
4. Divide batter evenly between the mason jars.
5. Pour 1-inch hot water into the dish surrounding the mason jars.
6. Bake for 45 minutes.
7. Allow cooling in the water before placing in the refrigerator.

SUGAR-FREE CHOCOLATE COVERED STRAWBERRIES

Ingredients 7 servings

- Sugar-free chocolate chips – ½ cup
- Coconut oil – 2 tbsp.
- Strawberries – 14
- Shredded unsweetened coconut or chopped nuts – ¼ cup

Method

1. Melt the coconut oil and chocolate chips in the microwave.
2. Stir until completely smooth.
3. Wash and dry the strawberries but leave the stem.
4. One by one dip the strawberries in the melted chocolate to coat.
5. On a parchment lined baking sheet, place the coated strawberries.
6. Sprinkle the nuts or coconuts and let sit for 10 minutes to harden.

NO SUGAR CHOCOLATE CAKE

Ingredients for 6 servings

- Unsweetened baking chocolate – 7.5 oz.
- Unsweetened cocoa powder – 1 tbsp.
- Baking soda – ½ tsp.
- Pitted dates – 1 ¼ cup
- Eggs – 3 large
- Coconut oil – ¼ cup
- Vanilla extract – 1 tsp.

Method

1. Preheat the oven to 350F.
2. Pulse cocoa powder, chocolate and baking soda in a food processor and pulse until the texture of coarse sand.
3. Pulse pitted dates, then eggs, vanilla, and coconut oil.
4. Into an 8x8 inch baking dish, transfer the batter.
5. Bake until a toothpick comes out clean, about 25 minutes.
6. Cool before serving.

NO ADDED SUGAR DATE BARS

Ingredients for 1 square

Dry

- Oats – 1 ½ cup (divided)
- Unsweetened coconut – ½ cup
- Medjool dates – 5
- Walnuts – ½ cup
- Sea salt – ¼ tsp.
- Baking soda – ½ tsp.
- Egg – 1
- Ground flax – 2 tbsp.
- Coconut oil – ¼ cup

Date layer

- Medjool dates – 18
- Lemon juice – 1 tsp.
- Sea salt to taste

Method

1. Preheat the oven to 325F.
2. In a food processor, add 1-cup oatmeal and process until a flour forms.
3. Add baking soda, sea salt, dates and coconut, and process until dates are fully broken up.
4. Add walnuts and other ½-cup oatmeal. Pulse until walnuts are chopped, but a bit chunky.
5. To the food processor bowl, add coconut oil, flax, and the egg, pulse until combined.
6. Reserve ½ cup of oatmeal mixture to use as a topping.

7. Line an 8 x 8 pan with baking paper.
8. Add the rest of the oatmeal cookie mixture to the pan. Press down to make an even layer.
9. Add date layer ingredients in a clean food processor and pulse until the dates are broken up. Then process until dates take on a light, whipped caramel color.
10. With wet hands, add the date later on top of the cookie layer.
11. Then crumble the reserved ½ cup of oatmeal mixture over the top.
12. Bake for 18 minutes.
13. Completely cool and slice.

SUGAR-FREE PEACH ICE CREAM

Ingredients for 2 servings

- Frozen peach slices – 2 cups
- Coconut milk – ¼ cup plus 1 tbsp.
- Mint sprigs and or diced peaches for garnish

Method

1. In a food processor, place the frozen peaches and process for 5 minutes or until peaches have started to break down.
2. Add the coconut milk and process until the mixture is creamy.
3. Spoon the mixture into bowls.
4. Garnish with mint and diced peaches.

SUGAR-FREE MOUSSE AU CHOCOLOVE

Ingredients for 1 or 2 servings

- Ripe avocado – 1 large (halved, pitted and flesh scoop out)
- Medjool dates – 1, pitted (pitted and peeled)
- Raw cacao powder – 1 tbsp.
- Vanilla powder or vanilla extract – 1/8 tsp.
- Cinnamon – 1/8 tsp.
- Nut milk – ¼ cup
- Himalayan or sea salt – 1 pinch
- Mesquite powder – 1 tsp.
- Carob powder – 1 tsp.

Method

1. Add all the ingredients to a food processor and blend until smooth. Add more liquid if needed.
2. Serve.

SUGAR-FREE BERRY FROZEN YOGURT

Ingredients for 24 ounces

- Frozen berries – 2 cups
- Plain yogurt – 1 cup
- 1% milk – ½ cup
- Ice – 1 cup
- Vanilla liquid stevia – 4 droppers full
- Toppings – chopped nuts, chocolate chips

Method

1. In a blender, blend all the ingredients.
2. Once mixed, add the mixture to the ice cream machine and follow instructions of manual.
3. Serve.

SUGAR-FREE CHOCOLATE CHIP COOKIES

Ingredients for 1 ½ dozen

- Ripe bananas – 2
- Oats – 1 ½ cups
- Peanut butter – ½ cup
- Chocolate chips – ¼ cup

Method

1. Preheat the oven to 350F.
2. With parchment paper, line one or two baking sheets.
3. Except for the chocolate chips, mix all the ingredients in a bowl.
4. Then fold in the chocolate chips.
5. Onto the prepared baking sheet(s), drop batter by tablespoons.
6. Bake until bottoms and sides are golden browns, about 10 to 12 minutes.
7. Cool completely and serve.

NO-SUGAR AVOCADO CHOCOLATE PUDDING

Ingredients for 5 servings

- Pudding ingredients
- Dates – 10, pitted and roughly chopped
- Coconut water – ½ cups
- Bananas – 2 ripe
- Avocado – ½, pitted and scooped
- Unsweetened almond butter – ¼ cup
- Unsweetened cocoa powder - ¼ cup

Garnish

- Unsweetened coconut flakes – 1 tbsp.
- Blueberries – ¼ cup
- Strawberries – ½ cup, sliced
- Banana – 1, sliced
- Mint sprig

Method

1. Blend dates with half of the coconut water in a blender until smooth.
2. Add other half of the coconut water and rest of the ingredients. Blend until smooth.
3. Fill a bowl with ½ cup of the pudding.
4. Garnish with garnish ingredients.
5. Serve.

CONCLUSION

The book includes a variety of mouthwatering dessert recipes for every season. All recipes are made without added sugar, yet look and taste delicious. Your whole family will enjoy the recipes.

Copyright 2017 by Olga Reed - All rights reserved.

All rights Reserved. No part of this publication or the information in it may be quoted from or reproduced in any form by means such as printing, scanning, photocopying or otherwise without prior written permission of the copyright holder.

Disclaimer and Terms of Use: Effort has been made to ensure that the information in this book is accurate and complete, however, the author and the publisher do not warrant the accuracy of the information, text and graphics   contained within the book due to the rapidly changing nature of science, research, known and unknown facts and internet. The Author and the publisher do not hold any responsibility for errors, omissions or contrary interpretation of the subject matter herein. This book is presented solely for motivational and informational purposes only.

Printed in Great Britain
by Amazon